MORRIS J. SUGARMAN

Historian's Notebook:

Student Workbook to
THE HOLOCAUST

**The World and the Jews,
1933–1945**

BEHRMAN HOUSE, INC.

ACKNOWLEDGMENTS

I would like to express my thanks to several people who have helped me in the preparation of this workbook: Ilene McGrath, who read the original manuscript and made significant improvements; Sharmila Chanderdat and Janice Clonmell, my former students, who typed successive drafts of the manuscript with such patience, competence, care, and unremitting good cheer; and my colleague, David Klein, who lent a sorely needed helping hand when several technical problems took a turn for the chaotic. And I am particularly grateful to David Behrman, latest in the line of excellent editors with whom I have worked at Behrman House, whose guidance of the project has been informed by a rigorous professional standard, clarity of purpose, intellectual flexibility and unfailing sensitivity.

Finally, I would like to pay personal tribute to the textbook's author and my first editor at Behrman House, Seymour Rossel—writer, editor, consummate teacher, and a singular force of energy in the field of Jewish education. Working with him on our many projects has been, for me, an ongoing learning experience and a constant source of joy.

—M.J.S.

Cover and Book Design by Richard Stalzer Associates, Ltd.
Published by Behrman House, Inc.

ISBN: 0-87441-531-4

For Mel,

Whose warmth, wisdom, integrity, and humor
have meant so much to me over the years.
A special person.
A very special friend.

CONTENTS

I
STUDYING THE HOLOCAUST

Scanning
The Sources

Study the photograph on pages 14-15 and the table on page 16. These are your sources. On the basis of what you observe, mark each of the statements below **T** (True) or **F** (False).

_____ **1.** The overwhelming majority of Jews killed in the Holocaust came from the countries of Eastern Europe.

_____ **2.** The Germans waged war not only against rival armies, but against civilian populations as well.

_____ **3.** The Germans showed more compassion to women and children than they did to men.

_____ **4.** Few Scandinavian Jews were murdered in the Holocaust.

_____ **5.** The Jews in the photograph did not know whether they would live or die from day to day, or even from minute to minute.

_____ **6.** Only German soldiers who were also Nazis knew of and participated in the persecution of European Jews.

A Historian's Observations

The history of the Jewish people is marked by both triumph and tragedy. The triumphs have their roots in many different areas, but the tragedies usually come out of persecution. Below is a list of holidays, events, and institutions connected with the persecution of Jews—along with a historian's observations describing these terms. Place the number of the term in the left column next to the observation referring to it in the right column.

1. **Pesah**

2. **Purim**

3. **The Spanish Inquisition**

4. **Ghetto**

5. **Tisha B'Av**

6. **Hanukkah**

7. **Kiddush Hashem**

8. **Pogrom**

_____ "Established to insure that Jews will be set apart physically, religiously, and culturally from their neighbors."

_____ "Commemorates the destruction of both the First and Second Temples in Jerusalem."

_____ "This enslaved people lived as a peaceful and productive community for centuries. Their ancestor once saved the country from famine and starvation—a fact that the ruler has chosen to ignore. I think that what the government wants is an unending supply of slave labor."

_____ "This persecution was both political and religious. But there were also two miracles marking Jewish victory over this persecution—one military, the other religious."

_____ "This is the worst of all. These are their neighbors. They do business with one another. And then one fine day, maybe because they are bitter, angry, or frustrated, these neighbors decide to burst into the Jewish quarter, to loot, to burn and destroy, and to break heads."

_____ "Strange! Here is a people, and a tradition, that cherishes life. And yet on occasion, an act of suicide in the name of religious integrity or political freedom is praised as something sanctified and holy."

_____ "This is the first instance of modern anti-Semitism. The Jews were strangers, a minority in someone else's country, dependent upon others' good will for their safety and security. Then someone in power decided to murder them, and whether or not they survived was largely a matter of luck."

_____ "So much for the 'Golden Age.' Centuries of social contribution and cultural achievement mean nothing in the face of religious intolerance. Poetry and philosophy are no defense against expulsion and being burned at the stake."

Ideas And Meanings

Use the material in Chapter I and your general knowledge to answer the following questions.

1. What does the word "Holocaust" mean to you, and why do you think it is used?

_____

_____

_____

2. Why is it important to study history firsthand, from actual sources?

_____

_____

_____

3. Why do some people insist that the Holocaust never happened, or try to play down its seriousness?

_____

_____

_____

4. How would you explain the Jewish tradition that when a life is taken, an entire world is lost?

_____

_____

_____

5. Why are there no fathers or strong young men in the photograph on pages 14-15 ?

_____

_____

_____

Personal Responses

1. "Look, the Holocaust happened decades ago. Why are we so concerned with ancient history? Now is what is important, not then."

AGREE ☐   DISAGREE ☐

REASON _____

_____

_____

2. "'Nazi' refers to a political party; 'German' refers to a whole people. Therefore, the Holocaust should be described as German, not just Nazi."

AGREE ☐   DISAGREE ☐

REASON _____

_____

_____

3. "The Holocaust could happen only in a dictatorship, never in a democracy."

AGREE ☐   DISAGREE ☐

REASON _____

_____

_____

4. "The Holocaust is not just a Jewish concern; it is a human concern. It touches everyone."

AGREE ☐   DISAGREE ☐

REASON _____

_____

_____

5. "The Holocaust could never happen again."

AGREE ☐   DISAGREE ☐

REASON _____

_____

_____

Then
And Today

However else you may describe the Holocaust, it represented a total disregard for human life. Can you think of any similar disregard today? Explain the similarities, and the differences.

_____

_____

_____

_____

_____

_____

_____

_____

_____

_____

_____

_____

_____

_____

_____

II
THE HOLOCAUST BEGINS

Looking Backward

Historians see events through the eyes of people who were there. Today it is easy to say, "Why didn't the Jews of Germany leave when they had the chance?" But what was it actually like for the Jews? All but one of the statements below might have been made by a Jew in Hitler's Germany during the 1930s. Circle the number before the statement that could *not* have been made, and explain why.

1. "Germany is my country. My roots go back hundreds of years. I speak the language. I know the culture. This is where I belong."

2. "The Nazis want us to leave. I flatly refuse to play into their hands."

3. "Hitler and his gang are just a temporary evil. When the people of Germany come to their senses, they will throw these low-lifes out of power."

4. "This anti-Semitism is limited to a tiny minority of top officials. Ordinary Germans don't feel that way. On a day-to-day level, I have no problems. I go to theaters, concerts, restaurants, and resorts; my children have no trouble at school."

5. "Sure they expelled the Polish Jews, but these people were foreigners. The Nazis wouldn't dare do that to native-born German Jews."

6. "I have too much invested here . . . my home, my business, everything I have worked for . . . ."

EXPLANATION _____

_____

_____

_____

_____

Examining The Evidence

History is not only about *what* happened, but also about *how* and *why*. The best evidence comes from primary sources—actual data such as letters, photographs, diaries, official documents, newspaper accounts, and recorded conversations. Below are three groups of statements, each drawn from a specific primary source in the chapter. For each group, circle the letter before the statement that you believe is *not* supported by the evidence. Then give a brief reason for your choice.

1. From Zindel Grynszpan's account on pages 20-21, we learn that
   a. the Jews who were sent back to Poland arrived in a state of desperate poverty.
   b. the SS guards believed that they could be as brutal as they pleased to departing Polish Jews.
   c. the Polish authorities proved to be every bit as merciless as the Germans.
   d. the Germans devised laws to enable them to rob the Jews of their wealth and property "legally."

   REASON _____
   _____
   _____
   _____
   _____

2. From the four photographs in the chapter, we learn that
   a. German Jews made no significant contribution to the country's economy.
   b. German Jews actively and openly practiced their religious tradition.
   c. the Nazi authorities were determined to isolate the German Jews from the population at large.
   d. the Nazis encouraged random acts of violence against Jews and their property.
   e. the Nazis showed neither concern nor respect for Jewish religious settings.

   REASON _____
   _____
   _____
   _____
   _____

3. From the Nazi messages and conversations on pages 22-23, 24-25, 26, and 27, we learn that
   a. the Nazi leaders didn't consider the Jews to be "real" Germans.
   b. without the murder of von Rath, the Nazis could never have convinced the German people to commit violence against the Jews.
   c. business people, as well as ordinary civilians, actively participated in the anti-Jewish aktionen.
   d. the Nazis originally wanted to drive the Jews (but not their wealth) out of Germany.

   REASON _____
   _____
   _____
   _____
   _____

Contradictions

The Holocaust is marked by contradictions. Complete each of the statements below with a specific contradiction drawn from the material in the chapter.

1. Jews had lived in Germany for many centuries. They spoke the language, were rooted in the culture, contributed to the society and economy, and yet _____

_____

_____

_____

_____

2. Germany was a Western society, very much like our own. It was highly developed, with a strong scientific and intellectual tradition, an educated population, and a network of laws, and yet _____

_____

_____

_____

_____

3. German Jews lived side by side with their non-Jewish neighbors. They knew each other, did business together, sent their children to the same schools, and yet _____

_____

_____

_____

_____

Seeking Out Symptoms

We have all heard of AIDS, the terrifying illness that destroys the body's immune system and leaves the individual defenseless against disease. German Jews of the 1930s were stripped of their political immune system, robbed of the civil and human rights that most of us take for granted. What would it be like to be part of a community afflicted with political AIDS? See if you can find a "symptom"—that is, a specific example of the breakdown of German Jewish rights—in each of the following areas.

1. The right to personal safety and protection against physical assault.

_____

_____

_____

2. The right to protection of wealth and property.

_____

_____

_____

3. The right to due process of law and protection against unlawful arrest.

_____

_____

_____

4. The right to a good name—protection against slander and libel.

_____

_____

_____

5. The right to equality before the law and protection against discrimination.

_____

_____

_____

6. The right to free religious expression.

_____

_____

_____

7. The right to life, liberty, and the pursuit of happiness.

_____

_____

_____

A Personal Journal

We have learned a great deal about the Holocaust from the personal journals of its victims. Imagine that you are a Jewish teenager living in Germany during the 1930s. Write an entry in your personal journal, describing an event that would have meaning to you. You might want to recall a family discussion. Or something that happened in school. Or on the street. Or any other situation that you can think of.

_____

_____

_____

_____

_____

_____

_____

_____

_____

_____

III
LIFE IN THE GHETTOS

Textbook
Pages 30-41

Conflicting Views

The Jews under German occupation were often forced to make agonizing choices. The following exchange between a father and his daughter could have taken place in any of the ghettos. The father has been asked to serve as a member of the *Judenraete*. He is inclined to accept, but his daughter bitterly objects. You are a family friend. Express your own opinion, and explain why.

THE FATHER'S POSITION:

■ "Our community needs organization and leadership. The *Judenraete* gives us both."

■ "Our most important goal is survival. We want to keep our people alive for as long as possible. If cooperating with the Germans helps achieve this, we have to do it—as distasteful as that may be."

■ "I worry about the children. They are so young, so vulnerable, so defenseless. And they are our future. The *Judenraete* will allow us to set up hospitals, clinics, and schools for them."

■ "Working with the Germans means creating relationships—lines of communication—which may encourage them to soften their policies."

THE DAUGHTER'S POSITION:

■ "You are playing their game, doing their dirty work, ultimately making their job easier."

■ "When you cooperate with the Germans, you are saying that what they are doing is acceptable and legitimate. I cannot agree. We must reject their programs and resist them in every way we know how."

■ "In the end, everyone will hate you. Our people are so sick, so scared, so hungry. They want someone to blame, someone to hate. They'll accuse you of abusing your power and living high off the hog while everyone else suffers. Won't that kind of thing divide us, turn us against each other?"

YOUR POSITION _____

_____

YOUR REASON _____

_____

_____

_____

In Addition

The **historian** is also a detective, using "clues" to develop new insights. Examine the insights drawn from each of the sources noted below, and then add one or more of your own.

1. From Heydrich's memo on page 30, we learn that
   a. the Nazis had formulated a long-term approach to the "Jewish Question."
   b. this approach would entail a great deal of work and careful organization.
   c. the Jews were to be isolated from the non-Jewish population.

IN ADDITION _____

_____

2. From the map on page 32 and the photographs on pages 31, 33, 35, 36, 38, and 40, we learn that
   a. Germany and Russia cooperated with one another in the early stages of the war.
   b. the Jews were forced to participate in their own isolation and imprisonment.
   c. suffering, starvation, and death were constant elements in the life of the ghetto.
   d. The Jews were determined to create some form of "normal" life for their children.

IN ADDITION _____

_____

3. From the diaries of Hirszfeld on page 33, and Ringelblum on page 34, we learn that
   a. the German guards were capable of acts of great cruelty.
   b. the children were also exposed to terror and death on a daily basis.
   c. the Jews felt a strong sense of responsibility for one another.

IN ADDITION _____

_____

Observations

An outsider visiting the Warsaw Ghetto in 1942 could have made the following observations. All of them but one would have been accurate. On the basis of the facts in the chapter, circle the number before the observation that is *not* accurate, and give the reason for your choice.

1. "Many of the inhabitants are sick and starving."

2. "I have literally seen people die before my eyes."

3. "I found a copy of an underground newspaper, printed in Yiddish and Hebrew."

4. "I passed a cellar window, and I could swear that I heard a Hebrew prayer."

5. "There are so many children—very little children—wandering the streets, lost and abandoned."

6. "Would you believe it? Someone told me that one of the inhabitants is giving a violin concert!"

7. "I saw two German soldiers shoving an old man. Later on, they beat him to the ground."

8. "There is no sense of community here. Everybody seems to be going his or her own way."

9. "I saw a group of young Jews being led out of the ghetto—part of a labor gang, I would guess."

10. I went down to a basement. There was a gray-haired man sitting next to a teenage boy. They were going over the Torah portion for the boy's Bar Mitzvah."

REASON _____

_____

_____

_____

A Declaration of Spiritual Resistance

To the Nazis, the Jews were less than human. Many Jews responded by defiantly asserting their humanity through spiritual resistance. Find a photograph or another primary source in Chapter III which illustrates how each of the following expressions of spiritual resistance was carried out.

1. We will live a Jewish life no matter what the risk!

   _____

2. We will continue reading and thinking!

   _____

3. We will take care of our fellow Jews as best we can—particularly the children

   _____

4. We will instill in our children the hope for a future of peace and freedom, and we will prepare them to take part in that future!

   _____

5. We will celebrate the joyous occasions of our lives!

   _____

6. We will create islands of intellectual activity and cultural beauty in this sea of ugliness and death.

   _____

Interpretations

Review the story of Janusz Korczak on page 37. It has been widely heralded as an example of moral greatness.

1. Why does he say that "man is a creature of understanding and goodness. Not just 100, but 150 [children] are in the Dom Sierot [orphanage]"?

_____

_____

_____

_____

2. Why, when he was ordered to take the children to Treblinka, did he dress them in their best _shabbat_ clothing and lead them singing through the streets of Warsaw?

_____

_____

_____

_____

3. What does the story of the crippled child with one eye tell us about Korczak's character?

_____

_____

_____

_____

IV
THE DEATH CAMPS

Textbook
Pages 42-53

Causes and Consequences

History is a chain of causes and consequences. Place the number of each cause next to its consequence.

CAUSE

1. To justify his planned destruction of Jewish people . . .

2. Because the Nazis wanted to make their program of mass murder more efficient . . .

3. Because the Nazis wanted to begin a large-scale extermination program quickly . . .

4. Because local populations in places like Lithuania and the Ukraine were so anti-Semitic . . .

5. Because Hitler wanted the German people to be not only racially pure, but also physically perfect . . .

6. Because the German guards were taught that the Jews were less than human . . .

7. Because the work of the *Einsatzgruppen* was going too slowly . . .

8. Because the Nazis needed slave labor . . .

9. Because the Nazis wanted to prevent Jewish resistance . . .

10. Because the Nazis wanted to profit from these mass murders . . .

CONSEQUENCE

_____ they moved almost all Jews to larger cities and put them in ghettos.

_____ the Nazis recruited them to help German guards force Jews to the death camps.

_____ the Nazis decided to use poison gas as their method of mass murder.

_____ they made a great effort to deceive their victims until the last minute.

_____ Hitler told lies to make it seem that the Jews were responsible for the outbreak of World War II.

_____ they ordered that 3,000 *Einsatzgruppen* follow the German army into Russia to execute Jews.

_____ they devised an elaborate system of stealing every valuable item that the Jews owned.

_____ most of them were able to beat the Jews and force them to their deaths with little feeling of guilt or regret.

_____ he ordered a program of "mercy killing" (euthanasia) in which handicapped children were put to death.

_____ they created a program called "the Selection," in which they would choose strong young men to work while sending the rest of the Jews to their deaths.

21

"Only Professionals Need Apply"

Historians of the Holocaust have long puzzled over such questions as "Who knew?" "How many knew?" and "How much did people really know?" But one point is beyond dispute: many well-educated, highly trained professionals were involved. Without them, the death camps could not have been built and the mass murders could not have been carried out.

Each of the "Help-Wanted" cards below and on the next page could have been posted on the bulletin board of the local German labor exchange. The title of the job is at the top. You fill in the "Job Description." Be factual, be accurate, and do not mince words.

HELP WANTED

JOB TITLE:

Physician

_____

JOB DESCRIPTION: _____

_____

_____

_____

_____

_____

HELP WANTED

JOB TITLE:

Transportation Expert

_____

JOB DESCRIPTION: _____

_____

_____

_____

_____

_____

HELP WANTED

JOB TITLE:

Dentist

_____

JOB DESCRIPTION: _____

_____

_____

_____

_____

_____

HELP WANTED

JOB TITLE:

Public Relations Writer

_____

JOB DESCRIPTION: _____

_____

_____

_____

_____

_____

"Only Professionals Need Apply" (continued)

HELP WANTED
JOB TITLE:
Architect
_____

JOB DESCRIPTION: _____
_____
_____
_____
_____
_____

HELP WANTED
JOB TITLE:
Administrator
_____

JOB DESCRIPTION: _____
_____
_____
_____
_____
_____

HELP WANTED
JOB TITLE:
Jeweler
_____

JOB DESCRIPTION: _____
_____
_____
_____
_____
_____

HELP WANTED
JOB TITLE:
Engineer
_____

JOB DESCRIPTION: _____
_____
_____
_____
_____
_____

Reasons And Responses

Imagine that the war has just ended. You meet a doctor who worked in one of the death camps. You want to know how he could have committed these crimes. These are his reasons. How would you respond to each one?

1. "I didn't make the rules. I didn't set policy. I was just a professional hired to do a job, and I did it as best I could."

YOUR RESPONSE _____

_____

_____

2. "My country was at war. I was called upon to serve, so I did my patriotic duty. Wouldn't you have done the same?"

YOUR RESPONSE _____

_____

_____

3. "War is brutal. People get killed. Members of my family and my friends were killed by your bombs. Why don't you condemn your own pilots and soldiers? Why do you set us apart as something evil?"

YOUR RESPONSE _____

_____

_____

4. "Everyone was involved. If I had not done it, someone else would have—so what difference does it make in the end?"

YOUR RESPONSE _____

_____

_____

5. "For years, it was drummed into our heads to hate the Jews. They were our enemies. And in time of war, you kill your enemies!"

YOUR RESPONSE _____

_____

_____

The Making of a Nazi

Nazis were not born, they were made. Take a long look at the various Nazis in the photographs on pages 43, 46, and 48. They seem like ordinary people, yet they committed unspeakable crimes. What ingredients do you think went into the making of a Nazi?

Below are a number of ingredients—social, economic, intellectual, personal—that influenced Germans to join the Nazi Party. Examine them, and describe how each one helps make a Nazi.

INGREDIENT	IMPACT
1. A poor education.	
2. Financial insecurity.	
3. Low self-esteem; unstable family.	
4. The need to find a scapegoat to blame and to hate.	
5. Nazi propaganda—symbols, ceremonies, rallies, weapons, patriotic pride.	

Finally, complete this statement: *A Nazi is an individual who*

_____

_____

_____

_____

About
The Photographs:
Facts and Meanings

The photographs in this chapter call to mind a statement made by a historian who said, "The more I know about the Holocaust, the less I know about the Holocaust." Still, we must keep trying to know—and to understand. One of the ways that historians develop understanding is by examining facts. Each of the following photographs conveys a fact. Examine each photograph, and write down what for you is its most important meaning.

1. **FACT:** Jews stripping and shivering, awaiting execution while the German guards chatter away. (Page 46).

MEANING _____

_____

_____

_____

_____

2. **FACT:** German guards supervising and organizing the Hungarian Jews arriving at Auschwitz. (Page 48).

MEANING _____

_____

_____

_____

_____

3. **FACT:** Women and children, part of the column scheduled for immediate execution. Look at their faces, at the yellow star, at the smallest children. (Page 49).

MEANING _____

_____

_____

_____

_____

4. **FACT:** Assorted valuables taken from the victims. (Page 50).

MEANING _____

_____

_____

_____

_____

5. **FACT:** Bodies on their way to the ovens, and the ovens themselves. (Pages 51, 52).

MEANING _____

_____

_____

_____

_____

V
WHY THE JEWS?

A Dictionary of Anti-Semitism

Help develop a dictionary of anti-Semitism. Each of the descriptions below is a definition; see if you can identify what each one is defining.

1. The Nazi newspaper whose objective was to stir up hatred of Jews.

_____

_____

_____

_____

2. The accusation that Jews observe Passover by murdering non-Jews—most often, children.

_____

_____

_____

_____

3. The word that means "to judge without proving," which has been responsible for so much fear, suspicion, hatred, and human suffering.

_____

_____

_____

_____

4. The Christian armies that banded together in the Middle Ages to try to capture the Holy Land. They were unsuccessful, but they plundered and massacred many Jewish communities along the way.

_____

_____

_____

_____

5. The founder of Protestantism who, when the Jews refused to convert to his new religion, turned against them and became an aggressive anti-Semite.

_____

_____

_____

_____

6. The name of any general characteristic attributed to *all* members of a particular race, religion, or ethnic group.

_____

_____

_____

_____

Profile of A Pathology

Anti-Semitism is a pathology—a deeply destructive social illness that goes back more than 2,000 years. Using the material in this chapter, as well as your general knowledge, see if you can create a profile of anti-Semitism by briefly explaining each of the following categories.

THE ROOT CAUSES OF ANTI-SEMITISM

1. **Political causes:**

   _____

   _____

   _____

2. **Economic causes:**

   _____

   _____

   _____

3. **Cultural causes:**
   (habit and tradition)

   _____

   _____

   _____

4. **Psychological causes:**
   (suspicion and superstition)

   _____

   _____

   _____

DIFFERENT FORMS OF ANTI-SEMITISM

1. **Religious anti-Semitism**

   _____

   _____

   _____

   _____

   _____

2. **Racial anti-Semitism**

   _____

   _____

   _____

   _____

   _____

   _____

CONTEMPORARY INSTANCES OF ANTI-SEMITISM	MAJOR CONSEQUENCES OF ANTI-SEMITISM
1. Anti-Semitism in this country _____ _____ _____	(Not all consequences need be negative. For example, one major modern consequence was the mass immigration of Eastern European Jews to the United States.) **1.** _____ _____ _____
2. Anti-Semitism abroad (particularly in Eastern Europe) _____ _____ _____	**2.** _____ _____ _____
3. Anti-Semitism expressed through anti-Israeli attitudes and actions _____ _____ _____	**OTHER** _____ _____ _____

Historical Fact-Finding

Support each of the general statements below with a specific event, photograph or other fact from the chapter (for many, there are several from which to choose).

1. Through the centuries, the Jewish people have held on to their special religious and cultural tradition despite many pressures.

_____

_____

2. One of the major ingredients of anti-Semitism has been a superstitious fear of the unknown.

_____

_____

3. In the years before World War II, German Jews believed that they were a part of German national life and culture.

_____

_____

4. Church leaders hated the Jews for rejecting Christian religious teachings.

_____

_____

5. During the Middle Ages, Church authorities physically isolated the Jews and made them second-class citizens.

_____

_____

6. Superstitious accusations concerning Jewish ritual murder practices were expressed long before the birth of Christianity.

_____

_____

7. Many Christians from the Middle Ages showed little concern for Jewish lives.

_____

_____

8. Racial anti-Semitism proved to be even more threatening and frightening than religious anti-Semitism.

_____

_____

9. Higher education and professional training did not guarantee that a person would reject Nazi doctrine.

_____

_____

10. Anti-Semites of both the racial and religious varieties tried to destroy sources of Jewish learning.

_____

_____

11. Some Jews tried to hide or deny their Jewish identity.

_____

_____

A Family History

Prejudice and persecution have often forced Jews to flee to new lands. Look into your own family's history to see if your relatives fled persecution. Here are some of the questions you might ask your parents, your grandparents, or other relatives.

1. Where do we come from? _____

   _____

2. How long had our family lived there? _____

   _____

3. When did we leave? _____

   _____

4. Why did we leave? _____

   _____

5. Where did we live when we first arrived here? _____

   _____

6. How did we support ourselves? _____

   _____

7. What kind of synagogue did we belong to? _____

   _____

8. Have you ever experienced prejudice or
   discrimination in this country? If so, describe it. _____

   _____

9. Do you feel secure here? Why, or why not? _____

   _____

Insights
And Impressions

This exercise contains three statements made in response to photographs and illustrations in the book. Read each statement. Look at the photographs and illustrations. Then add an insight or impression of your own.

1. From the Bull of Pope Julius calling for Talmud-burning (page 60) and from the photograph of Nazi book-burning (page 60), we learn that the authorities used symbols of church and state to justify their acts of destruction.

   AND . . . (your insight or impression)_____

   _____

   _____

2. From the photograph of Yom Kippur services in the German Army (page 64), we learn that German Jews fought in that country's army.

   AND . . . _____

   _____

   _____

3. From the photograph of *Der Sturmer* featuring a ritual murder (page 62), the Nazi beer coaster (page 65), and the young couple at an anti-Semitic exhibition (page 66), we learn that the Nazis mounted a mammoth propaganda campaign against the Jews.

   AND . . . _____

   _____

   _____

Looking Inward

In a way, the anti-Semite and the committed Jew agree on one point: Jews *are* different. But the committed Jew believes that Jews should *strive* to be different. Look at your own Jewish life—at the traditions you observe, the values you cherish, the concerns you share with other Jews in your community and around the world.

1. Do you believe that Jews *are* different—truly set apart from their non-Jewish neighbors? Explain why, or why not.

_____

_____

_____

_____

2. What are the distinctive features of your Jewish identity?

_____

_____

_____

_____

3. What do you like most about being Jewish?

_____

_____

_____

_____

4. What do you think is most difficult about being Jewish?

_____

_____

_____

_____

Over the Breakfast Table

When we think of *Der Sturmer* today, we recognize it as an obscene promoter of lies, hatred, and violence. But how did the average German feel? Imagine that you are that average German, looking at the morning paper, and that your younger brother or sister sees the photograph on page 62 and asks you to answer the following questions.

1. Who are the Jews in the picture?

_____

_____

_____

2. What are they doing?

_____

_____

_____

3. Why are they doing it?

_____

_____

_____

Then one of your parents asks you two other questions.

1. What does the photograph teach you about Jewish religious practices?

_____

_____

_____

2. How does this make you feel about Jews?

_____

_____

_____

VI
THE NAZI RISE TO POWER

From the Historian's Notebook

Identify the following.

1. The World War I treaty that made Germans feel bitter and betrayed.

   _____

2. Hitler's expert in propaganda.

   _____

3. The name of Hitler's first attempt to take political power, for which he was sent to prison.

   _____

4. The book Hitler wrote in prison.

   _____

5. Hitler's second-in-command and head of the *Luftwaffe,* the German air force.

   _____

6. The law that transferred power from the *Reichstag* to Hitler.

   _____

7. The Nazi term for pure-blooded Germans.

   _____

8. The head of the SS, who also commanded the program to destroy the Jews of Europe.

   _____

9. The idea that expressed the need for more German "living space," to be taken from other people's lands.

   _____

10. The Nazi colonel who was captured and tried as a war criminal in Israel in 1961.

   _____

The Reasons Why

Complete each of the following statements.

1. The German authorities ordered "un-German" books to be burned in Berlin because _____

_____

_____

_____

2. Military officers supported the Nazi Party because _____

_____

_____

_____

3. Business leaders supported Hitler's rise to power because _____

_____

_____

_____

4. Poor people and members of the working class voted for the Nazi Party because

_____

_____

_____

_____

5. Hitler organized the Night of the Long Knives because _____

_____

_____

_____

6. Anti-Semitism was a key element of the program of the Nazi Party because

_____

_____

_____

_____

7. Karl Lueger's religious anti-Semitism was not strong enough for Hitler because

_____

_____

_____

_____

39

Chain of Consequences

Major historical events have chains of many consequences. For each event below, circle the letter before each of the consequences of the event; *one* statement in each group *is not* a consequence. Then describe which consequence you think was the most serious, and explain why.

1. ***The Treaty of Versailles***
   a. humiliated most Germans.
   b. contributed to the German government's instability.
   c. created a deep German hatred of all things French.
   d. made many Germans openly sympathetic to Nazi ideas and ambitions.
   e. helped bring about World War II.

   MOST SERIOUS _____

   EXPLANATION _____

   _____

   _____

   _____

2. ***The Great Depression of 1929***
   a. dramatically worsened the German economy.
   b. drove many Germans to emigrate to the United States.
   c. caused thousands of Germans to lose their jobs.
   d. strengthened Hitler's hand and helped make the Nazis a major force in German politics.
   e. intensified German feelings of anti-Semitism.

   MOST SERIOUS _____

   EXPLANATION _____

   _____

   _____

   _____

3. ***The Reichstag fire***
   a. created tension between Germany and Holland.
   b. gave Hitler an excuse to imprison thousands of political enemies.
   c. helped bring about the elimination of all German civil and human rights.
   d. helped make the Nazi party all-powerful.
   e. helped make Hitler the absolute dictator of Germany.

   MOST SERIOUS _____

   EXPLANATION _____

   _____

   _____

   _____

Ideas And Meanings

Explain the following.

1. Heinrich Heine wrote that "where books are burned, in the end men will burn as well." What exactly does he mean? How would this happen? Do you agree or disagree with what he says? Why? _____

_____

_____

_____

_____

_____

_____

2. It has been said that a disastrous economy actively threatens the very survival of a democracy. Why would this be the case? Do the events in Chapter VI support this idea? Why? _____

_____

_____

_____

_____

_____

_____

Finding The Evidence

Each of the following statements is derived from primary source material in the chapter. Find a source that supports or illustrates each statement (for example, a specific photograph or quote). If there are several sources, choose the most important two or three.

1. Anti-Semitism was deeply rooted in German and Austrian culture.

   SOURCE _____

   _____

2. Early Nazis looked and acted like average people.

   SOURCE _____

   _____

3. Part of the Nazi formula for success was hard work and painstaking organization.

   SOURCE _____

   _____

4. Hitler was a spellbinding speaker who could convey his message to vast audiences.

   SOURCE _____

   _____

5. Hitler pursued power aggressively and ruthlessly.

   SOURCE _____

   _____

6. During the early 1930s many Germans were poor and felt helpless.

   SOURCE _____

   _____

A Mosaic of Anti-Semitism

Anti-Semitism is like a mosaic made up of different fragments. Write in all the factors you can think of that contribute to anti-Semitism. If you have more causes than fragments, then simply draw another line and create a new fragment. Compare your mosaic with those of your classmates.

VII
PEOPLE WILL BELIEVE WHAT THEY ARE TOLD

A Museum Tour

Nazi propaganda was highly effective; it mesmerized and mobilized tens of millions of Germans. Below are eight statements which could be made by a tour guide in a Museum of Nazi Propaganda. Find in Chapter VII a reference to — or a photograph of — each piece of propaganda being described by the tour guide.

1. "This man first put propaganda on the map. He recognized its political possibilities and made it a major center of power within the government."

   _____

2. "Look at them. Tall, blond, blue-eyed, athletic, disciplined, dressed in simple uniforms, and thoroughly patriotic."

   _____

3. "This so-called children's book was a runaway best seller. An innocent German girl—foolish but virtuous. A fat, ugly, menacing Jewish doctor. Finally, a happy ending, Nazi style! Talk about stereotypes!"

   _____

4. "This journalist was the worst! His anti-Semitism, his capacity for sheer hatred, and his ability to portray the Jew in absolutely obscene terms knew no bounds. He used old religious themes to stir up hatred. And his newspaper was a classic example of anti-Semitic literature."

   _____

5. "This little gadget helped change the world. It became a standard piece of furniture in every German living room and gave Hitler a ready-made audience, not of thousands, not of ten thousands, but of _millions!_"

   _____

6. "I hate to say it, but this is a great documentary. It makes fascinating viewing even today. And it reveals the power of pageants and parades and uniforms and flags to inspire and unite."

   _____

7. "This demonstrates the dark side of the propaganda film. You watch this movie, and you walk out absolutely hating anybody remotely Jewish."

   _____

8. "The Nazis weren't religious, but they didn't mind using religion to achieve their goals. The custom I am about to show you is pure paganism. Instead of a big statue of wood and stone, they come and worship a portrait!"

   _____

The Reasons Why

Complete the following statements.

1. The Nazis made propaganda a major priority because _____

_____

_____

_____

_____

2. German women were encouraged to stay at home and have many children because _____

_____

_____

_____

_____

3. The Nazis encouraged boys and girls to join youth movements because _____

_____

_____

_____

_____

4. The Nazis made sure that cheap radios were available in stores because _____

_____

_____

_____

_____

5. The Nazis blacklisted thousands of books and organized book-burnings throughout Germany because _____

_____

_____

_____

_____

6. Albert Speer believed that the Nazis had more influence and power than any government ever had because _____

_____

_____

_____

_____

7. Hitler believed that effective propaganda must be confined to a very few points and must be repeated endlessly because ____

_____

_____

_____

_____

Notes From a Nazi Curriculum

The Nazis quickly assumed control of the national educational system. Each of the statements below describes a subject that might be included in the Nazi curriculum. However, at least one of them is an educational "subversive," which might undermine Nazi political objectives. Circle the number before each statement that you believe could be subversive, and then explain why.

1. "A course in German History focusing on our past glories and highlighting our heroes."

2. "Courses in Math and Science, producing a generation of scientists and engineers."

3. "A course in Physical Education, producing strong, healthy men and women."

4. "A course in German Music and Poetry, giving us an appreciation of our tradition and culture."

5. "A course in Composition, giving our young people the ability to read with logic and express their thoughts clearly."

6. "A course in a foreign language, enabling our young diplomats to function effectively."

EXPLANATION _____

_____

_____

_____

_____

_____

A Blueprint Of Human Needs

The Nazi propaganda machine understood human nature and created programs that fitted specific human needs and desires. For each need or desire below, write in a Nazi activity that fulfilled it.

THE NEED AND DESIRE	THE ACTIVITY
1. To belong	_____ _____
2. To achieve self esteem	_____ _____
3. To worship	_____ _____
4. To hate	_____ _____
5. To fulfill a purpose	_____ _____
6. To be excited	_____ _____
7. To develop pride	_____ _____
8. To obey	_____ _____

In Addition

Examine the insights that are drawn from each of the sources below. Then add one of your own.

1. From the memoir of the boy who joined the Hitler Youth (page 87), we learn that
   a. not everyone who became a member was a full-fledged Nazi.
   b. the Nazis knew how to create an attractive social atmosphere to appeal to German young people.

IN ADDITION _____
_____
_____
_____

2. From Albert Speer's observations (page 93), we learn that
   a. mass communication is a powerful political weapon.
   b. technology can help bring about political revolution.

IN ADDITION _____
_____
_____
_____

3. From the photographs of Goebbels (page 83), and Hitler (pages 90, 91), we learn that
   a. they looked remarkably *unlike* the image of the ideal German man that they tried to promote.
   b. Hitler wanted to portray himself as a man of the people.

IN ADDITION _____
_____
_____
_____

4. From the photograph of the young homemakers (page 84) and the illustration of the Hitler youth (page 87), we learn that
  a. Nazi propagandists favored outdoor, country settings.
  b. the Nazis encouraged the youth to look alike and dress alike.

IN ADDITION _____

_____

_____

5. From the photograph advertising the film *Jud Suss* (page 89) and the excerpt of *The Poisonous Mushroom* (page 86), we learn that
  a. the Nazis went to great lengths to stir up hatred of Jews.
  b. they portrayed Jews as a dark, physically repulsive, violent presence—the very opposite of the ideal German.

IN ADDITION _____

_____

_____

6. From the film *Triumph of the Will* (pages 90-91), we learn that
  a. the Nazis used visual images very effectively.
  b. the Nazis understood the vast appeal of ritual and ceremony.

IN ADDITION _____

_____

_____

Creating Pride

Imagine that

The year is 1939. You are a Jewish teenager, still living in Germany. Your parents have been trying to leave, but they cannot find a country to go to. So you wait . . . The whole country is abuzz with excitement—rallies, parades, uniforms, banners, Hitler youth outings—but you are totally left out. Your friends and neighbors want nothing to do with you.

Your little brother comes in the room. He is in tears. He has no more friends. People point to him, make fun of him, and call him names. "You know," he exclaims bitterly, "I hate being Jewish. Look at what's happened to us! Why can't we just be like everyone else?"

You need to teach him. What would you say to him? Which aspects of Jewish history, laws, and values make you proud? How would you go about making him proud to be a Jew in the face of a relentless propaganda machine that teaches exactly the opposite?

I WOULD SAY TO MY LITTLE BROTHER _____

_____

_____

_____

_____

_____

_____

_____

VIII
NO WAY OUT

Textbook
Pages 94-101

A Barrier Of Beliefs

German Jews during the 1930s held many beliefs that persuaded them to remain in Germany until there was no way out. Explain how each of the beliefs below helped prevent Jews from leaving, and whether it is similar to any of your beliefs today.

1. A belief in their German roots.

_____

_____

_____

2. A belief in their constitutional rights.

_____

_____

_____

3. A belief in German-Jewish history.

_____

_____

_____

4. A belief in their non-Jewish neighbors.

_____

_____

_____

5. A belief in logic, law, and order.

_____

_____

_____

On the Move: Postmarks

As the Nazis grew more violent, European Jews searched urgently for places of refuge. Families split up but desperately tried to stay in contact with one another. The only way to do this was through the mail. Listed on the next page are some of the places where Jews found themselves, and excerpts of letters from these places which could have been written by Jews on the move. Figure out where each was written, and fill in the city name in the appropriate postmark.

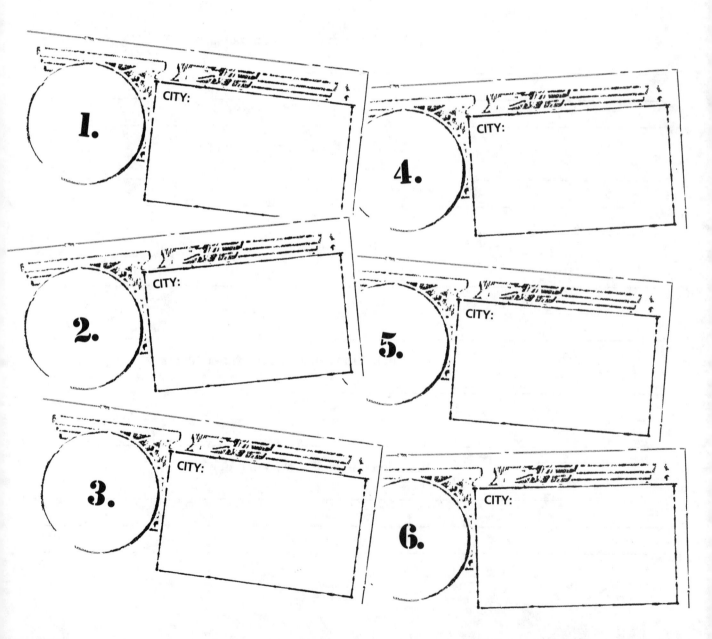

1. CITY:

2. CITY:

3. CITY:

4. CITY:

5. CITY:

6. CITY:

LETTERS AND PLACES

1. "Dear children, I am glad that you are out and safe. I wouldn't want you to pay the price of my stubbornness. But this is where I was born. This is my country. My culture. My language. I fought with the army."

2. "An ocean's a wonderful thing! It's as though Hitler and the Nazis never existed. But the people in this country are living in a dream world where nothing bad can ever happen. And they are suspicious of immigrants and want to severely limit their number."

3. "I feel strange here, but thank God for their hospitality. It's crazy! I am driven from my home, my country, my very life—everything that means anything to me—in the name of a racist doctrine. And here I find refuge with people of another race."

4. "The funny thing is, I never felt really Jewish. And here I am with Jews from so many different countries. All of us learning a new language, trying to communicate with one another. I'll tell you one thing: It's as though I've come home—really come home—for the first time in my life."

5. "I don't understand these people. They talk at you in bureaucratic mumbo-jumbo and say absolutely nothing. They refer to rules and regulations, and when I spoke of all those people drowning, they shrugged their shoulders. 'Not our responsibility,' they insisted."

6. "These people are out and out crooks! They took our money, and then they went back on their word. It's as if they were talking about cargo—only the cargo is human lives. And they come down to stare at us every day. Our pain, our fear, is their circus."

Shanghai

Jerusalem

New York

Havana

Berlin

Istanbul

Scanning The Sources

Support each of the statements below with a specific reference to a photograph or quotation in Chapter VIII. There may be several pieces of evidence—choose the strongest in each case.

STATEMENT

EVIDENCE

1. Many German Jews belonged to the middle class.

2. German Jews felt at home and secure in Germany for a long time.

3. Strong religious faith can be a source of comfort and courage.

4. The Jews learned that they could not depend upon outsiders for help.

5. German Jews felt that they were patriots and valuable contributing citizens.

6. When confronted with danger, German Jews often denied (to others and to themselves) that things were really as bad as they seemed.

7. Many German Jews affirmed their Jewish identity and tradition, even in the face of misfortune.

Then and Now: Business as Usual

The Jews of Europe had no way out because the world practiced "business as usual." The British practiced *politics as usual*, severely limiting Jewish immigration to Palestine for fear of upsetting the local Arab population. The United States practiced *economic and domestic policy as usual*, worrying about the impact of immigrants on the job market and playing up to isolationist sentiment. Cuba and Turkey practiced *bureaucracy as usual*. The nations of Europe, among other things, practiced *anti-Semitism as usual*. And many German Jews practiced *yesterday as usual*, saying, "This is where I always lived and where I always will live. I am sure that things will get better."

Can you point to any "as usual" situations today—those in which people ignore great danger and tragedy? In this country? In Israel? Elsewhere? Write down one strong example. Why do you think it is important? Why do people so often respond to serious challenges and crises with "business as usual"?

EXAMPLE _____

_____

_____

_____

IMPORTANCE _____

_____

_____

_____

_____

REASON FOR A "BUSINESS AS USUAL" MENTALITY _____

_____

_____

_____

_____

_____

True or False

Mark **each** of the statements below **T** if true, **F** if false, or **I** if there is insufficient information upon which to base a judgment.

_____ 1. German Jewry had a clear-cut community structure.

_____ 2. German Jews were indifferent to Zionism because they were afraid that their non-Jewish neighbors would question their patriotism.

_____ 3. Jews began to feel the anti-Jewish laws soon after the Nazis assumed power.

_____ 4. In their rush to assimilate, most German Jews rejected their religious heritage.

_____ 5. In pre-Nazi Germany, Jews were largely confined to ghettos.

_____ 6. Many German Jews escaped Germany only to have the Holocaust catch up to them later.

_____ 7. Anti-Semitism was the major reason Cuba broke its promise and made the Jews' landing certificates invalid.

_____ 8. Individual Jews tried to help the Jews of Europe.

_____ 9. The British White Paper prevented many Jews from escaping from the Holocaust.

_____ 10. Many Germans went out of their way to protect their Jewish friends and neighbors.

_____ 11. German Jews demonstrated much courage, optimism, and faith.

IX
THE WAR AND THE JEWS

Textbook Pages 102-113

From the Underground: Radio Waves

The radio was a key factor in the outcome of the Second World War. For the Nazis it was an instrument of mass propaganda, and for millions of people caught in Europe it was the only means of contact with the outside world.

The following excerpts could have been taken from radio transcripts made by the anti-Nazi underground before and during the war. Some of them were cause for despair; others, for hope. Identify the event or idea to which each of the transcripts below refers.

1. "This is unbelievable! The greatest rescue operation in history—a victory by air and by sea, directly defying a vast, brutal military machine."

   _____

2. "This so-called doctrine is nothing more than the justification of a land-grab, a return to the law of the jungle. What the Germans are saying is, 'This is what we need, so we'll take it, regardless of anyone else's rights'."

   _____

3. "This will finally bring America into the war and help turn the tide."

   _____

4. "The Nazis took a gamble and they won! They broke international law, violated their own commitments, and dared the nations of the world to stop them. Do you really think that they'll stop here? This is the first step on the road to war."

   _____

5. "This is a whole new concept of war. Time is transformed. We see before us not so much a battle, but a clean sweep in a matter of days!"

   _____

6. "This is the day that the free world has been waiting for. A day of sacrifice! A day of hope! And for the Nazis, the invasion marks the beginning of the end!"

   _____

7. "Everyone anticipated this attack; we just weren't sure when it would take place. Now Hitler may learn—as Napoleon did more than a hundred years ago—that the biggest military obstacle is sometimes not an enemy army but the weather!"

   _____

Insights And Impressions

The world of Anne Frank no longer exists, but we have records—photographs, documents, and above all her diary. Using these various sources, what can we learn about her world?

1. Look closely at the photograph of Anne Frank (page 107). Study her face, her posture, her expressions. What are your impressions of her? What kind of person does she strike you as being?

2. On the basis of what she writes (pages 107-12), what do you think her family was like? Her growing-up years? What were the values that were most important to her?

3. She and her family lived in a constant shadow of danger, terror, and death. How did she deal with this situation?

4. What did she mean by "What one Christian does is his own responsibility, what one Jew does is thrown back at all Jews" (page 111). Do you think that this is true today?

5. She described her experiences in vivid terms. Write down some of the frightening sights and sounds that she encountered on a daily basis.

Examining Sources: General and Specific

For each of the following statements, identify a specific photo or diary entry that supports it.

1. The war between the German army and its enemies was absurdly unequal.

   _____

2. The Germans waged war not only against opposing armies, but against civilian populations as well.

   _____

3. The Germans treated the Jewish population with consistent brutality and without regard to personal dignity or to human life.

   _____

4. Terror could occur in seemingly normal surroundings.

   _____

5. Many Jews were keenly aware of what awaited them in concentration camps.

   _____

6. The Frank family tried to preserve a sense of normal life and hope in the face of an ongoing nightmare.

   _____

7. Anne Frank wanted the world to know and remember the suffering of the Jews.

   _____

Strategy For Survival

Imagine that you are part of a group of Jewish teenagers hiding from the Nazis in the cellar of a Christian couple. You are confined to two tiny rooms. You must work out a strategy for survival: you have to live together, share what you have, keep tensions down, be sensitive to health needs, and create a daily routine that will make life bearable.

In the space below, write what you consider to be the best possible strategy for survival. What are the greatest dangers? What steps can be taken to avert these dangers?

STRATEGY _____

_____

_____

_____

DANGERS _____

_____

_____

_____

STEPS TO AVOID DANGERS _____

_____

_____

_____

_____

Photo Study: What Can We Learn?

Examine carefully the photographs on pages 103, 104, 105 and 106. What can we learn about the following?

1. The power and extent of the German military machine.

_____

_____

_____

_____

2. The strength and level of preparation of the Polish army.

_____

_____

_____

_____

3. Human bravery in battle.

_____

_____

_____

_____

4. The will to survive in the face of impossible odds.

_____

_____

_____

_____

The Lessons of History

History can be a teacher. Write a lesson that we can draw from each of the following events.

1. The events that preceded the outbreak of World War II.

LESSON _____

_____

_____

_____

2. The experience of the German army in Russia.

LESSON _____

_____

_____

_____

3. The evacuation of Dunkirk.

LESSON _____

_____

_____

_____

4. The negative change in attitude toward the Jews by many Dutch citizens.

LESSON _____

_____

_____

_____

5. The fanatic determination of the Germans to destroy Europe's remaining Jews, even in the face of their own defeat.

LESSON _____

_____

_____

_____

X
RESISTANCE

A Historical Review

Identify the following.

1. The Hebrew word for "holocaust," and its meaning.

   _____

2. The term used in the concentration camps for an individual who lost all hope and all will to survive.

   _____

3. The five keys to survival within the camps.

   1. _____

   2. _____

   3. _____

   4. _____

   5. _____

4. The most famous ghetto uprising—a model of Jewish heroism and resistance ever since World War II.

   _____

5. The name for the freedom fighters who hid in the forests and attacked German troops whenever and wherever possible.

   _____

6. The name of the Jewish woman who became a symbol of courage for the Jews in Auschwitz.

   _____

Interpretation: Poem of Resistance

The poem by Hirsh Glik (pages 118-19) is a prime example of spiritual resistance. Read it carefully. Listen to its words and to its rhythms. Then answer the following questions.

1. What is its overall message?

_____

_____

_____

2. Which of its phrases and images express the need for hope?

_____

_____

_____

3. The author mentions a number of colors. What qualities of life (or death) does each of these colors represent?

_____

_____

_____

4. A particularly vivid expression of faith can be found in the words "But if the sun delays and in the east remains— This song as slogan, generations must maintain." Can you explain its meaning?

_____

_____

_____

5. What is your interpretation of the stanza that begins "This song written with our blood, not with lead"?

_____

_____

_____

6. Which lines in the poem move you the most emotionally? Why?

_____

_____

_____

The Reasons Why

Complete **each** of the following statements.

1. The organizers of revolts were mainly young Socialists, Communists, and Zionists because _____

_____

_____

2. Immediately after the war there was little evidence of Jewish resistance because _____

_____

_____

3. The Jews in the ghettos had more reason to hope than those in the concentration camps because _____

_____

_____

4. Jews with strong religious or political commitments seemed better able to survive than those who did not because _____

_____

_____

5. Many Jewish leaders in the ghettos believed it was better to cooperate with the Germans than to revolt because ___

_____

_____

_____

Refuting Lies

Because Jewish resistance in the Warsaw ghetto embarrassed them, the Germans invented a number of lies to minimize that embarrassment. For each of the following German lies, find a piece of primary evidence in Chapter X that refutes it, and explain why.

1. "German soldiers fought heroically against great odds."

_____

_____

_____

2. "Our soldiers would never harm women, children, or old people."

_____

_____

_____

3. "The Jews were weak and cowardly. Polish partisans did their fighting for them."

_____

_____

_____

4. "Once we recovered from their surprise attack, we defeated the resistance very easily."

_____

_____

_____

A Ghetto Journal

The Time: January 1943

The Place: The Warsaw Ghetto

The Characters: Young, active members of the Zionist movement, determined to resist further Nazi moves against the 70,000 remaining Jews.

The Plot: One of the group announces: "I've had only limited luck purchasing guns, but look at what I found—a printing press! It's old, it's rickety, it smears, but it works. Let's put out a ghetto journal—to inform, to inspire, to unite, and to communicate with the remaining remnant of Jews scattered throughout the ghetto."

In the space below, make a brief contribution to this journal—a story, an editorial, a poem, a cartoon. Remember that this journal can be a spiritual and psychological lifeline to thousands of abandoned Jews.

GHETTO JOURNAL

Impressions

1. Most of the concentration camps and ghettos were located in Poland. ____

2. More revolts took place in ghettos than in concentration camps. ____

3. The Germans showed more compassion to women and children than they did to men. ____

4. The Jews frequently fought the Germans in the face of almost impossible military odds. ____

5. Religious Jews opposed armed resistance to the Germans. ____

6. Jewish partisans frequently fought side by side with Russian and Polish partisans. ____

7. Jewish women fought as bravely and effectively as men. ____

8. The majority of Jews who participated in revolts and partisan raids survived. ____

9. The Warsaw ghetto uprising was a source of inspiration to European Jews. ____

10. The Warsaw ghetto uprising was a source of embarrassment to the Germans. ____

XI

WHEN DID THE WORLD LEARN OF THE HOLOCAUST?

Textbook
Pages 130-139

Rationalization And Response

How would you respond to the following explanation for the media's lack of attention to human suffering? Could it include the Holocaust? Could it include other events?

66My business is selling the news. I focus upon what I think my audience will be interested in. If I bore them (with tragedy after tragedy), I'll lose them.99

_____

_____

_____

_____

How would you respond to the following rationalization for the failure of the Allies to take additional steps to save Europe's Jews?

66Everything you are asking for in the name of humanitarian rescue efforts would either prolong or complicate the war effort. You want to bomb railroad routes to concentration camps? That would divert our air power from military targets. You want to ransom Romanian Jews? You are putting money into the hands of the enemy. You want to rescue refugees? Where would we put them? How could we feed them? Rescue through military victory is the best plan.99

_____

_____

_____

_____

"Business As Usual" Continued

An earlier chapter spoke of "business as usual" — people responding to sudden danger with conventional reactions. Briefly describe the "business as usual" approach of the following responses to the Holocaust. How was it "business as usual"? What were the reasons for this reaction?

1. Holocaust coverage by the news media (pages 130-36).

_____

_____

_____

2. The U.S. State Department's response to Riegner's telegram (pages 133-36).

_____

_____

_____

3. The refusal of the Allies to ransom 70,000 Romanian Jews (page 136).

_____

_____

_____

4. The policy of "rescue through victory" (page 136).

_____

_____

_____

5. The responses by Hebrew newspapers in Palestine and by the Jewish Frontier to early reports of atrocities against the Jews (page 131).

_____

_____

_____

6. President Franklin Roosevelt's statement on page 134.

_____

_____

_____

Historical Fact-Finding

Support each of the following general statements with a specific fact from the chapter.

1. American Jews never hesitated to express their open and active opposition to Nazi policy.

   _____

   _____

   _____

2. Evidence of German atrocities against the Jews was available from the very early years of the war.

   _____

   _____

   _____

3. A number of government leaders believed that helping the Jews could hurt the war effort.

   _____

   _____

   _____

4. The magnitude of Germans crimes was so vast that many people—including Jewish leaders—could not truly comprehend what was happening.

   _____

   _____

5. Some high government officials hesitated to help rescue the Jews because of political and economic convenience.

   _____

   _____

   _____

6. Many American Jewish leaders were not sure of how best to help European Jews.

   _____

   _____

   _____

7. Jews in Europe felt abandoned by the world at large and by their fellow Jews.

   _____

   _____

   _____

8. To some extent, the inaction of the world could be described as a failure of imagination. People simply could not grasp its reality until they saw for themselves, and then it was too late.

   _____

   _____

   _____

Ideas And Meanings

How would you interpret the meaning of the following?

1. The "for sale" ad (page 136). (Do you think that this is a straight advertisement, or does it contain bitter sarcasm?)

_____

_____

_____

_____

_____

2. Felix Frankfurter's response to Jan Karski (page 138).

_____

_____

_____

_____

3. The statement of the Warsaw ghetto fighters that Jewish leaders would be uninterested in their struggle (page 137).

_____

_____

_____

_____

4. The *Jewish Frontier*'s description of Shmuel Zygelbojm's suicide (page 139). Why did he commit suicide? What did he hope to achieve?

_____

_____

_____

_____

Apply **Hillel's** three simple questions to the Holocaust. What lessons can be learned from each question? And to whom does each of these lessons apply?

1. "If I am not for myself, who will be for me?"

_____

_____

_____

_____

2. "If I am only for myself, what am I?"

_____

_____

_____

_____

3. "And if not now, when?"

_____

_____

_____

_____

Screaming In Silence

Look at the photograph of the *New York Times* report (page 135). What does it tell you about news priorities at that time. What kinds of stories are featured more prominently—and why? This is but a single example of how the news media played down the tragedy of European Jewry during the war. In effect, the ghetto fighters and Shmuel Zygelbojm were screaming in silence. The mass media are our window to the world. When they don't tell us something or when they play it down, we remain unaware, as though it had never happened.

Human suffering may take the form of epidemic illness, starvation, poverty, or military atrocity. Can you point to instances today of people screaming in silence, of human suffering that goes unnoticed? In Asia? In Africa? In Eastern Europe? In South America? In the Middle East? In this country?

Then and Today

Think about Edmund Burke's statement: "The only thing necessary for the triumph of evil is for good men to do nothing." How does this apply to the Holocaust? How might it apply to events taking place today?

TO THE HOLOCAUST	TO TODAY

XII

THE RIGHTEOUS FEW

Textbook Pages 140-151

A Rogues' Gallery Of The Righteous

In war, ideas of right and wrong can become perverted. For the Nazis the righteous Gentiles were not righteous at all. The following are descriptions of righteous Gentiles from a Nazi point of view. Interpret each description and write in the name of the righteous Gentile or Gentiles to whom it refers.

1. "A disgrace to his profession and to his so-called 'neutral' country. The word 'diplomat' should be changed to 'forger' and 'blackmailer'."

   _____

2. "What a poor example he must be to his students. An educator should educate, not become a smuggler of human cargo."

   _____

3. "In the end, blood is thicker than religious vows—which clearly means very little to him. All he seems to care about are Jewish children."

   _____

4. "This smuggler of children and procurer of arms is hardly a gentle lady of books. What's the matter with her?"

   _____

5. "Here's an example of collective hysteria if ever I saw one. One person. A second. A whole family. But in this case a whole town has gone mad."

   _____

6. "A forger, a smuggler, an all-around liar, who managed to corrupt other clergymen along the way!"

   _____

7. "The leadership of this country is in a state of total denial. How can he say there is 'no Jewish problem'? Every country has a Jewish problem. But if you tell a lie often enough, people begin to believe it."

   _____

Puzzles
And Paradoxes

Think about the following puzzles and paradoxes. Write down your ideas about them.

1. Why do some individuals respond heroically to crises while governments do nothing, even when they are well-intentioned? Think about the Allies' refusal to bomb Auschwitz, and the refusal of the British to exchange prisoners for 5,000 Jewish children. Contrast this to the actions of the righteous individuals.

_____

_____

_____

_____

_____

2. Why did the citizens of Denmark act with so much decency, courage, and compassion while citizens of other countries actively collaborated with the Nazis? What were the factors and forces that helped shape these responses?

_____

_____

_____

_____

_____

Quotations and Interpretations

Explain the meaning of each of the following statements.

1. "When the Germans forced Jews of Vilna into a ghetto, I could no longer go on with my work. I could not remain in my study. I could not eat. I was ashamed that I was not Jewish myself." Anna Semaite (page 142).

   Why was she unable to function normally? In what sense was she ashamed?

   _____

   _____

   _____

   _____

2. "None of us thought that we were heroes. We were just people trying to do our best." Magda Trocme (page 146).

   Why didn't the people of Le Chambon think that they were heroes? How would they have explained the words "trying to do our best"?

   _____

   _____

   _____

   _____

3. "Jewish problem—We have no Jewish problem in our country. The Jews are a part of the Danish nation." King Christian X (page 146).

   Why did the king say that there was no "Jewish problem"? Why did the Danes react so differently from most other Europeans?

   _____

   _____

   _____

   _____

4. "First they came for the Jews. I was silent. I was not a Jew. Then they came for the Communists. I was silent. I was not a Communist. Then they came for the trade unionists. I was silent. I was not a trade unionist. Then they came for me. There was no one left to speak for me." Martin Niemoeller (page 149).

Why were he and so many others silent? What might their voices have achieved, had they spoken?

_____

_____

_____

_____

A Value Search

The righteous individuals presented in this chapter were not born in a vacuum; their moral code and values made them act the way that they did. What are some of our most important Jewish values? Which Jewish values have made the greatest impact upon you—and why?

_____

_____

_____

_____

_____

_____

_____

The Lessons Of History

All but one of the following statements expresses a lesson of history from the narrative and the primary sources. Circle the number before the "lesson" that does not belong, and give the reason for your choice.

1. Every single country, even those with long histories of anti-Semitism, had righteous individuals willing to risk their lives for the Jews of Europe.

2. At times, a government or religious institution can become weighed down by traditional policies and procedures, unable to respond effectively to sudden crises or new moral challenges.

3. In moments of great need, many people find qualities of courage and principle that they did not know they had.

4. Acting morally can be more important than life itself.

5. Righteous individuals often identified strongly with the victims.

6. Evil can, at times, be so brutal and ruthless that it paralyzes all people, making them powerless to resist.

7. The Allied governments could have saved thousands of Jews.

8. At times, a group or a community acts heroically as a matter of moral conscience.

REASON _____

_____

_____

_____

Then and Today

"KOL YISRAEL AREVIM ZEH LAZEH"

The mission of the Jewish paratroopers behind enemy lines was twofold: first, to save as many Jews as possible; and second, to let the Jews of Europe know they were not alone, not abandoned.

This fundamental Jewish value is expressed in the Hebrew slogan above, which means "All of Israel (that is, the Jewish people) is linked to, and responsible for, one another."

The State of Israel was created both as a refuge and as a spiritual-cultural center to Jews the world over. Its most important precept is the law of the return, which means that any Jew who wants to come to Israel is automatically granted Israeli citizenship. Think about Israel's recent history. Identify two or three examples of how it has expressed this value in concrete terms to Jewish people or communities in need.

EXAMPLES _____

_____

_____

_____

_____

_____

_____

XIII A STRUGGLE TO THE DEATH

Textbook
Pages 152-163

The End And its Aftermath

To which person, place, or event does each of the following statements refer?

1. The location of the Allied invasion of Europe, launched on June 6, 1944.

   _____

2. The Germans' last attempt to hold off the American and British armies — the bloodiest battle of World War II.

   _____

3. The name of the "model ghetto" created by the Germans as a showcase concentration camp.

   _____

4. The name of the concentration camp that was the subject of a drawing depicting the arrival of prisoners.

   _____

5. The concentration camp in Germany where the British found 10,000 unburied bodies and where Anne Frank died in the final months of the war.

   _____

6. The name of the future Nobel Prize winning author who was among the survivors of Buchenwald.

   _____

7. The kind of dwelling, and the location, where Hitler hid and committed suicide in the final days of the war.

   _____ and _____

8. Three other groups of people who, like the Jews, were designated by the Germans for total extermination.

   _____,

   _____,

   and _____

9. The name for the camps set up by the British to hold Jews, who were not permitted to enter Palestine and who had no other place to go.

   _____

10. The name for the ship used to smuggle Jews from Europe to Palestine.

    _____

11. The date the United Nations voted to create the Jewish state, and the date Israel declared its independence.

    _____ and _____

A Photo Exhibit

The photographs in this chapter tell a moving story of the final days of the Holocaust and its aftermath. Each of the titles below refers to one of the photographs in the chapter. In the space beneath each title, write a phrase or sentence that explains what it is about.

1. The children of Theresienstadt (page 154).

EXPLANATION _____

_____

_____

2. Young survivors (page 159).

EXPLANATION _____

_____

_____

3. Arrival at Auschwitz (page 153).

EXPLANATION _____

_____

_____

4. Buchenwald (pages 156, 158).

EXPLANATION _____

_____

_____

5. The *Exodus* (page 160).

EXPLANATION _____

_____

_____

6. The birth of the Jewish State (page 161).

EXPLANATION _____

_____

_____

Stories And Insights

Each of the statements below offers an insight or idea into one of the stories told in the chapter. Read it, think about it, and then add an insight or insights of your own.

1. From the story about the "model ghetto," Theresienstadt (page 152), we learn that

   a. the Nazis practiced propaganda at home and "exported" it to audiences abroad.
   b. YOUR INSIGHT(S) _____

   _____

   _____

2. From the stories of the death marches (page 154-57), we learn that

   a. the Nazis wanted to hide their crimes.
   b. YOUR INSIGHT(S) _____

   _____

   _____

3. From the story of Israel Lau (page 155), we learn that

   a. even a very young boy can adapt and survive in brutal conditions.
   b. YOUR INSIGHT(S) _____

   _____

   _____

4. From the story of Levi Shalit (page 157), we learn that

   a. there is often a deep kinship between Jews.
   b. YOUR INSIGHT(S) _____

   _____

   _____

5. From the story of Hitler's final statement (pages 157-58), we learn that

    a. he blamed others for Germany's defeat even though he was its dictator.

    b. YOUR INSIGHT(S) _____

_____

_____

6. From the stories of Eastern European Jews who tried to return to their homes after the war (page 161) we learn that

    a. people can act with great brutality and violence, even after they have suffered themselves.

    b. YOUR INSIGHT(S) _____

_____

_____

7. From the stories of Displaced Persons (page 162), we learn that

    a. the Allied governments still conducted business as usual, despite the monumental human tragedy.

    b. YOUR INSIGHT(S) _____

_____

_____

8. From the quotation by Edward Yashinsky (page 162), we learn that

    a. the Jews of Europe felt a profound sense of abandonment.

    b. YOUR INSIGHT(S) _____

_____

_____

Then and Today

1. TELLING ABOUT THE PAST

The stories, diaries, drawings, and other evidence you have seen show the impassioned commitment of survivors to tell the story of the Holocaust. But a half-century has passed. Even the youngest Holocaust survivors are middle-aged, and the remaining Nazi war criminals are old and dying. How would you respond to the following statement?

"Enough already! It's time to forgive and forget! You are wallowing in the past. It is over! Most people today—including Germans—were born years after the Holocaust. So why the seminars and the courses? Why the memorials and the exhibits? Why the new books? You should focus on the present."

WHY?_____

_____

_____

_____

_____

_____

_____

_____

_____

_____

_____

_____

_____

_____

_____

2. ASKING IN THE PRESENT

Recounting the Holocaust calls to mind another act of telling: the Passover *Seder.* The *Haggadah* tells the story of the Exodus from Egypt, and it teaches us about freedom. One of the most important parts of the Seder is the traditional Four Questions, asked by the youngest child and answered by the leader of the Seder. It is a dialogue between one generation and the next.

You are part of the new generation. In the space below, write your own four questions about the Holocaust.

1. _____
_____
_____
_____

2. _____
_____
_____
_____

3. _____
_____
_____
_____

4. _____
_____
_____
_____

Exploring Motivations

The behavior of many German soldiers and civilians during the final days of the war was bizarre. The enemy was closing in, and surrender was only days away. Why did they persist in killing Jews? Why the death marches? On the basis of what you have read about the Nazis, and of your own instincts about human nature, why do you think the Germans failed to act in their own self-interest and either give up or run away?

WHY? _____

_____

_____

_____

_____

_____

_____

_____

_____

XIV
WAR CRIMES AND PUNISHMENT

Textbook Pages 164-177

People, Places, Facts and Ideas

Identify the following.

1. The name of the Allied court where German war criminals were tried.

   _____

2. The city in which the war crime trials were held.

   _____

3. The murderers and the victims in the first "crime against humanity" case early in the twentieth century.

   _____ and _____

4. The location of the Confederate prison camp whose commander had been tried for war crimes.

   _____

5. The three categories of crimes that the Germans were accused of committing.

   1. _____

   2. _____

   3. _____

6. The Latin name for the biblical principle of "life for life, eye for eye, tooth for tooth."

   _____

7. The German name for the defense that Hitler was the absolute dictator of Germany and that therefore those who obeyed his orders could not be held personally accountable for their actions.

   _____

8. The continent where many Nazis found refuge.

   _____

9. Two prominent individuals who dedicated their lives to tracking down Nazi war criminals.

   _____ and _____

10. The Nazi who was captured by Israelis, tried in Jerusalem, and executed for his crimes.

    _____

The Reasons Why

Complete the following sentences.

1. Three of the accused Nazi leaders were set free because _____

   _____

   _____

   _____

   _____

2. Most Americans eventually lost interest in the war crimes trials because _____

   _____

   _____

   _____

   _____

3. For many years after the war, the world was largely unaware of the "Final Solution" and other atrocities because _____

   _____

   _____

   _____

   _____

4. The Israelis kidnapped Eichmann rather than ask the Argentinians to arrest and extradite him because _____

   _____

   _____

   _____

   _____

   _____

5. Many Nazi scientists were welcomed by the American and Soviet governments because _____

   _____

   _____

   _____

   _____

6. Those hunting for Nazi war criminals blamed lack of progress in the United States on _____

   _____

   _____

   _____

   _____

Historical Fact-Finding

Illustrate each of the following general statements with a quotation from the text or with a reference to a photograph in the chapter.

1. The Allied armies were profoundly shocked by what they found in the death camps.

_____

_____

2. When it came to the Holocaust, Israel was more interested in the spirit rather than the letter of the law.

_____

_____

3. Many people (including leaders of governments) neither knew nor cared about the Holocaust.

_____

_____

4. The mass media can be a force both for good and for evil.

_____

_____

5. There were governments that placed political interests over moral considerations in dealing with the Holocaust.

_____

_____

Ideas
And Meanings

1. In your own words, briefly define the following terms, and give an example of each.
   a. Crimes against peace

DEFINITION _____

_____

EXAMPLE _____

_____

   b. War crimes

DEFINITION _____

_____

EXAMPLE _____

_____

   c. Crimes against humanity.

DEFINITION _____

_____

EXAMPLE _____

_____

2. On what grounds did the judges reject the defense arguments that accused Nazis were only following the orders of Hitler, who was the absolute dictator of Germany, and were therefore not personally accountable for their actions?

_____

_____

_____

3. Explain the distinction between simple justice and legal justice.

_____

_____

_____

4. Why do you think that the South American governments were hospitable to fleeing Nazi war criminals?

_____

_____

_____

5a. What does Israel's "Law of Judging Nazi Criminals and Their Helpers" say about its attitude toward human life?

_____

_____

_____

5b. About its view of the Holocaust?

_____

_____

_____

_____

_____

_____

Profiles

The **Nuremberg** and Eichmann trials profoundly affected world thinking. Examine the effects of each trial, and write down an additional important effect.

1. The Nuremberg trials
   a. provided a legal structure to express worldwide outrage at Nazi atrocities.
   b. established the principle of individual moral responsibility in times of war.
   c. AND _____

   _____
   _____
   _____
   _____
   _____
   _____

2. The Eichmann trial
   a. underscored Israel's role as agent of the worldwide Jewish community.
   b. dramatized the story of the Holocaust to the world at large.
   c. AND _____

   _____
   _____
   _____
   _____
   _____
   _____

The Definition of A Jewish State

When **Israel** passed the "Law of Judging Nazi War Criminals and Their Helpers," and later, when it brought Adolf Eichmann to trial, it was doing so not only for those who perished in the Holocaust, but in the name of Jews the world over. Israel, as someone once pointed out, is not just a state of Jews, it is a *Jewish state.*

What does the term "Jewish State" mean to you? What is the difference between a Jewish State and a state of Jews? How, specifically, does Israel express its distinctive Jewish identity, in terms of its history, its culture, its language, its religious tradition, its people, and its network of commitments?

_____

_____

_____

_____

_____

_____

_____

_____

_____

_____

_____

_____

_____